What is it?

 Colour the
pictures.

 Circle the
letters.

 Underline
the words.

a

apple

b

bunny

cat

c

 Let's start! At first, young children often confuse the terms 'letters' and 'words'. You can help by explaining that Letterland is a special place where all the letters live.

Meet the Letterlanders

Join each Letterlander to his or her letter.

Annie Apple

Bouncy Ben

Clever Cat

Listen

Here is a trick for discovering the sound each Letterlander makes in words. Just START to say a Letterlander's name, then STOP! Bouncy Ben says 'b...' rather than 'bee' or 'buh'.

Reading Direction

Trace the lines in the Reading Direction.

Look out for the red Reading Direction arrows in this book! They show our eyes and hands the way they need to move when we read and write. Ask your child to point out the Reading Direction when you read other books together.

Fred's fish tank

Circle two that are the same in each row.

Letter sounds

Firefighter Fred loves his fish tank, because it starts with his 'fff...' sound! Can your child spot anything in your home that starts with Fred's 'fff...' sound? (flowers, fork, food, five fingers, feet ...)

On the move

Circle four things that are different in the second picture.

Beginning sounds Ask your child to decide which Letterlanders might use each of these ways of getting around: train (Talking Tess), fire engine (Firefighter Fred), camel (Clever Cat), bus (Bouncy Ben).

Harry's hats

What words are missing?

Harry makes a lot of <u>h a t s</u>,

hats for ducks
and hats for _ _ _ _.

Even when Harry goes to _ _ _ _,

he still likes a hat upon his _ _ _ _ _.

Rhyming words

Ask your child which word you should write in each of the spaces provided. Can he or she tell you which word rhymes with hats (cats) and which word rhymes with bed (head)?

Rhyming riddles

Draw a line to the picture that completes the rhyme.

Tick tock, tick tock,
Sammy Snake has a ...

car.

Don't go too far,
Clever Cat, in your ...

dog.

Dippy Duck is on a log
playing with a little ...

sock.

Bim bam, bim bam,
Lucy has a little ...

lamb.

Nonsense rhymes

Have some fun with rhymes. Try making up nonsense words
that rhyme with both your names.

7

Blue balloons

Colour blue all the things that begin with Bouncy Ben's 'b...' sound.

Finish colouring the picture.

Sound & shape

Emphasise Ben's 'b...' sound as your child spots balloons, ball, bird and butterfly in the picture. Make a game of spotting Ben's small-letter shape on products and signs when you are out together.

Peter's picnic

Join Peter Puppy to the food that begins with his 'p' sound.

strawberries

pizza

pineapple

pear

carrot

banana

pie

apple

Letter shapes If your child confuses the **p** letter shape with **b** or **d**, tell him or her to notice how all three Letterlanders face in the Reading Direction. The one big difference is Peter Puppy's ears. They always droop down.

Same sounds

Circle the object that starts with the Letterlander's sound.

 t...

Talking Tess

 lll...

Lucy Lamp Light

 o...

Oscar Orange

 e...

Eddy Elephant

Together make the sound at the start of the Letterlander's name, e.g. 't...', not 'tuh' or 'tee'. Then say the name of each object, emphasising the first letter. For example, t...t...t, apple? No, that can't be right. t...t...tree? Yes! Circle it.

Match the letter pairs

Join the matching letters.

r

g

w

i

Explain that we cannot always see the Letterlanders in the writing that we see all around us, but we know they are hiding behind their plain letters, because we can still hear them making their sounds in words.

I-Spy

Tick the boxes as you find each thing in the big picture.

football ☐

cup ☐

hat ☐

frog ☐

Logic

Talk about the picture. The Letterlanders always love things that start with their sounds. Emphasise the first sound of each object in the side panels. Which Letterlander makes that sound? Look for each Letterlander and his or her object in the picture.

s

net ☐

horse ☐

cake ☐

nest ☐

Shadow fun

Join each Letterlander to his or her shadow.

Ask your child to choose a book. Select a page and then choose a letter. How many times can he or she spot that letter on the page?

Odd one out

Circle the odd one out in each line. What is missing?

your turn Have some fun and ask your child to draw three similar pictures, two the same and one slightly different so you can try spotting the odd one out!

15

Quarrelsome Queen's quilt

Look at the pictures carefully.

Circle four things that are different in the picture below.

Lore

Quarrelsome Queen is in her Quiet Room sewing a quilt. She always has her royal umbrella with her, wherever she goes. Can your child find the queen's royal umbrella in each picture?

Sammy's sandcastle

Look at the pictures and tell the story.

Reading Direction →

Colour the last picture.

Logic Remind your child that each Letterlander always loves things that start with their sound. Ask him or her to tell you which things in the pictures start with Sammy and Ben's sounds.

Letter sounds

Trace over the first letter in each big word.

 Annie Apple says 'a...' in the word ➡️ **ant.**

 Bouncy Ben says 'b...' in the word ➡️ **bus.**

 Clever Cat whispers 'c...' in the word ➡️ **cat.**

Dippy Duck says 'd...' in the word ➡️ **dog.**

 After you have read the sentence to your child, ask him or her to point to the letter in the word on the right that is making that Letterlander's sound (e.g. 'a...' as in 'ant'). The Letterlanders still make their sounds in these plain letters.

Eddy Elephant says 'e...' in the word →

egg.

Firefighter Fred whispers 'fff...' in the word →

frog.

Golden Girl says 'g...' in the word →

green.

Harry Hat Man whispers 'hhh...' in the word →

hat.

Act it out! Have some fun pretending to be a firefighter as you make Firefighter Fred's 'fff...' sound together. Encourage your child to say 'fff... fff... fff...'.

Letter sounds

Impy Ink says 'i...' in the word ➡ **ink.**

Jumping Jim says 'j...' in the word ➡ **jet.**

Kicking King whispers 'k...' in the word ➡ **kiss.**

Lucy Lamp Light says 'lll...' in the word ➡ **ladder.**

Same sound

Ask your child if they know which Letterlander on this page has the same sound as Clever Cat? It's Kicking King, of course!

Munching Mike says 'mmm...' in the word ➤ **milk.**

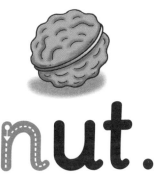

Noisy Nick says 'nnn...' in the word ➤ **nut.**

Oscar Orange says 'o...' in the word ➤ **on.**

Peter Puppy whispers 'p...' in the word ➤ **pink.**

Oscar's sound 🤝 Can your child think of a word that means the opposite of on and starts with Oscar Orange's sound? (off) Have fun stepping on and off a low step, saying 'on' and 'off' each time.

Letter sounds

Quarrelsome Queen says 'qu...' in the word →  **quilt.**

Red Robot says 'rrr...' in the word →  **ring.**

Sammy Snake hisses 'sss...' in the word → **sun.**

Talking Tess whispers 't...' in the word → **ten.**

Lore

Quarrelsome Queen never goes anywhere without her royal umbrella. That's why you will always see the letters qu together in words. They make a 'kw...' sound.

Reading Direction

Uppy Umbrella says 'u...' in the word  up.

Vicky Violet says 'vvv...' in the word van.

Walter Walrus says 'www...' in the word  web.

Fix-it Max whispers 'k-ss...' at the end of the word  box.

Letter sounds

Yellow Yo-yo Man says 'y...' in the word ➔ **yak.**

Zig Zag Zebra says 'zzz...' in the word ➔ **zip.**

Write your name on the dotted line.

is now ready to read!

Well done!

Well done!

When your child has finished the book, try going back over some of the activities he or she enjoyed most. You could also look at all the Letterlanders on the inside back cover and say their sounds together.